Whales

by Lesley A. DuTemple

Lerner Publications Company • Minneapolis, Minnesota

For my own pod: Jim, Margaret, and Chris
—L.A.D.

The photographs in this book are reproduced through the courtesy of: cover, © Michael Nolan/EarthViews; pp. 4, 6, 8, 20, © Douglas David Seifert/Tiny Bubbles Expeditions; pp. 7, 9, 14, 15, 16, 17 (inset), 25, 31, © Bob Cranston; pp. 10, 18, 27, 28–29, © Flip Nicklin/Minden Pictures; p. 11, © Steve McCutcheon/Visuals Unlimited; pp. 12, 24, 41 (bottom), 43, © Eda Rogers/Sea Images; pp. 13, 31 (inset), © Peter Howorth/Mo Yung Productions; p. 17, © Thomas Johnson/EarthViews; p. 18 (Inset), © Frank T. Awbrey/Visuals Unlimited; p. 19, © Richard Sears/EarthViews; pp. 21, 26, © Kevin & Cat Sweeney/Mo Yung Productions; p. 22, © Jim Harvey/Visuals Unlimited; pp. 30, 36, 46–47, 48, © Ron Sanford; pp. 32, 35, © John Hyde/Wild Things; pp. 33, 34, 37, © Cindy Kilgore Brown; p. 38, © Carlyn Galati/Visuals Unlimited; p. 39, © Bob Cranston/Mo Yung Productions; p. 40, © J. Michael Williamson/EarthViews; p. 41 (top), © Ernest H. Rogers/Sea Images; p. 42, © F. Stuart Westmorland/Mo Yung Productions

Thanks to our series consultant, Sharyn Fenwick, elementary science/math specialist. Mrs. Fenwick was the winner of the National Science Teachers Association 1991 Distinguished Teaching Award, She also was the recipient of the Presidential Award for Excellence in Math and Science Teaching, representing the state of Minnesota at the elementary level in 1992. And special thanks to our young helper, Ben Liestman.

Ruth Berman, series editor
Steve Foley, series designer

Library of Congress Cataloging-in-Publication Data

DuTemple, Lesley A.
    Whales / by Lesley A. DuTemple.
       p.   cm. — (Early bird nature books)
    Includes index.
    Summary: Describes the physical and social characteristics of various whale species, including the first year of a humpback whale calf.
    ISBN 0-8225-3008-2 (alk. paper)
    1. Whales—Juvenile literature. [1. Whales.] I. Title.
II. Series.
QL737.C4D835   1996
599.5—dc20   95-30803

Manufactured in the United States of America
1 2 3 4 5 6 – SP – 01 00 99 98 97 96

Contents

GREENLAND

Alaska
(U.S.)

CANADA

ICELAND

UNITED STATES

N

Hawaii
(U.S.)

CENTRAL
AMERICA

DOMINICAN
REPUBLIC

Humpback whales live in oceans all around the world. Two groups are shown on this map. One group swims between Alaska and Hawaii. The other group swims between Iceland, Greenland, and eastern U.S. to the Dominican Republic.

SOUTH
AMERICA

Be a Word Detective

Can you find these words as you read about the whale's life? Be a detective and try to figure out what they mean. You can turn to the glossary on page 47 for help.

baleen	echolocation	migrate
blowholes	ectotherm	plankton
blubber	endotherm	pods
breaching	fluke	

Chapter 1

A humpback whale leaps out of the water. Do you think whales have ever walked on legs?

Whales Walked Here

What animal weighs more than 25 elephants and has a tongue big enough for 50 people to stand on? What animal can hold its breath for 2 hours? And what animal looks like a fish, but isn't? If you guessed "a whale," you're right!

Whales have been around for millions of years. When dinosaurs lived on earth, whales walked on land. They had four legs then. They probably walked like alligators. Over thousands of years, whales' back legs disappeared. Their front legs changed to flippers. Whales started living in the water.

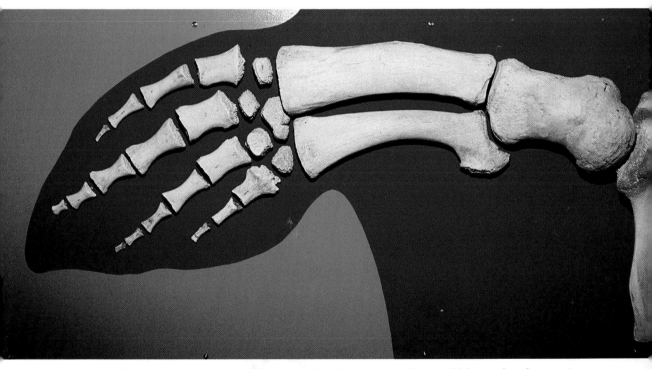

We know whales had lived on land because they still have leg bones in their bodies. And the bones in their flippers (above) *match the bones in a human arm and hand.*

Whales are mammals. Like all mammals, this young short-finned pilot whale (top) was born alive.

Although whales now live in water, they're not fish. Whales are mammals. Cats, dogs, and people are mammals, too. Mammals are animals who are born alive and drink their mother's milk. Most fish hatch from eggs. Then right away, they eat whatever they find in the water.

There are other differences between fish
and mammals. Fish are ectotherms (EK-toh-
therms), or cold-blooded. The temperature
inside their bodies changes with the temperature
of their surroundings. If the water they live in
is cold, their body temperature is cold.

*This sea bass is a fish. If the water surrounding the sea bass
is cold, its body temperature becomes cold.*

Mammals are endotherms (EN-doh-therms), or warm-blooded. That means their body temperature doesn't change much. A whale's body temperature stays the same whether it's swimming in icy oceans or warm oceans. People are endotherms too. Your body temperature is the same in winter and summer.

The tail of a humpback whale can be seen as it dives into icy waters.

The white blubber can be seen in a whale's flipper that has been cut up.

Mammals can be endotherms because our bodies have extra protection. You wear clothes to help you stay warm. Many other mammals have fur covering their bodies. Whales have blubber. Blubber is a thick layer of fat. Blubber helps whales stay warm even in cold water.

Fish have gills to help them breathe in the water. But mammals have to breathe air. They have lungs to help them breathe. Whales have to come to the surface to breathe, or they'll drown. Whales breathe through blowholes, or

Whales with teeth, like these killer whales, have one blowhole.

nostrils, that are on top of their heads. When whales swim to the surface, their blowholes open to let in air. When whales are ready to dive under water, their blowholes close so that no water gets into their lungs.

Whales without teeth, like this fin whale, have two blowholes.

Chapter 2

This sperm whale is a toothed whale. Can you name another kind of toothed whale?

Do Whales Have Teeth?

 There are more than 90 species, or kinds, of whales. We divide all whales into two main groups. One group is toothed whales. The other group is baleen (bah-LEEN) whales.

Toothed whales are predators, or hunters. They have teeth to help them catch fish and squid. Dolphins are toothed whales. Orcas, or killer whales, are a type of dolphin also. Orcas are the most popular of the toothed whales. Whales who do tricks in marine parks are usually orcas.

Toothed whales, like this killer whale, use their teeth only to catch the fish that they eat. They don't chew their food. Instead they swallow it whole.

Most toothed whales are small. Only one toothed whale, the sperm whale, is a giant. It's as big as a school bus. Sperm whales also have the thickest skin on earth. It's 14 inches thick!

Sperm whales are the biggest toothed whales. They can grow to be 60 feet long and weigh up to 60 tons.

Baleen can be seen hanging from the jaw of this gray whale's mouth.
Inset: *This is a close-up of a gray whale's baleen.*

Baleen whales are giants. But they are gentle giants without any teeth. Instead of teeth, they have plates of baleen. The baleen plates look like giant furry combs. They hang from a whale's upper jaw. The baleen plates are made of keratin. Your hair and nails are made of keratin, too.

Millions of plankton live in the ocean. Inset: *Krill are one kind of plankton that whales eat.*

Baleen whales eat plankton. Plankton are tiny plants and animals that float in the water. When a baleen whale opens its mouth to catch plankton, it also takes in a lot of water. The whale uses its tongue to push the water out of

*The blue whale, the largest animal on earth, can grow
to be 100 feet long and weigh 220 tons!*

its mouth. Plankton are trapped in the baleen,
then swallowed. The largest animal on earth,
the blue whale, is a species of baleen whale.
It's even bigger than the largest dinosaur that
ever lived!

Chapter 3

Whales can live from 15 to over 60 years depending on the species. This family of sperm whales may live to be over 60 years old. What are whale families called?

Whale Families

 Whales live and travel in family groups called pods. Pods can have a few members or hundreds of members. Toothed whales live in bigger pods than baleen whales. A pod of bottlenose dolphins may have 300 members. But a pod of humpback whales may have only 3 members. Humpbacks are baleen whales.

Pods are made up of bulls, cows, and calves. Bulls are male whales, cows are female whales, and calves are baby whales. A small pod has a mother, a father, and a baby. A bigger pod has mothers, fathers, and babies, too. But it also has grandparents, aunts, uncles, and cousins. Pod members communicate, or talk. They help each other just as human family members do.

A bull, cow, and calf make up this humpback whale pod.

Whales communicate by clicks, squeals, moans, and barks. They talk all the time. The ocean is full of their voices. Male humpback whales even sing. They can make about 1,000 different sounds. Each pod of humpback whales has its own special song.

Some whales can see very well. But they use their ears more than they use their eyes. A whale makes a sound. The sound hits an object

A friendly gray whale swims up to scientists who are recording whale sounds.

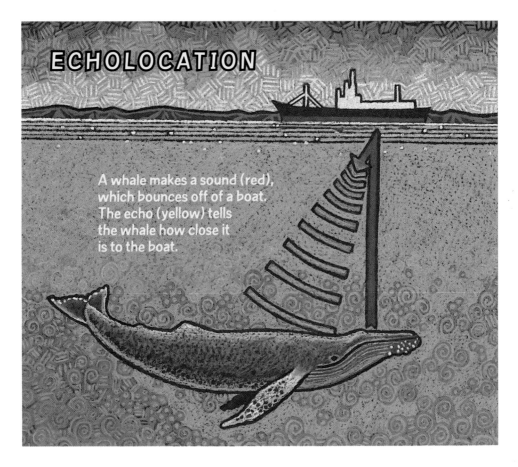

ECHOLOCATION

A whale makes a sound (red), which bounces off of a boat. The echo (yellow) tells the whale how close it is to the boat.

and bounces back to the whale. The sound that bounces back is called an echo (EH-koh). If the echo comes back fast, the whale knows the object is close. If the echo takes a long time to return, the object is far away. This special way of using echoes is called echolocation (eh-koh-loh-KAY-shen).

The ear opening of this pilot whale can be seen below its eye.

Whales use echolocation to find out what's around them. They can find out how deep the water is, how close the nearest whale is, or how big a boat is. They even use echolocation to find their food. Whales' ears are just two tiny holes in their skin, but they can hear sounds 1,000 miles away!

Chapter 4

Humpback whales travel long distances every year. Do you know when they migrate?

A Humpback Calf's First Year

 Baleen whales migrate, or travel when the seasons change. In the summer, they migrate north to find food. In the winter, they migrate south so their calves can be born in

A humpback cow and her calf swim in warm water.

warm, safe waters. Calves don't have much blubber, so they need to be in warm water. Toothed whales don't seem to migrate as baleen whales do.

Most whales, both toothed and baleen, start their lives in the same way. Humpbacks are baleen whales. This is the story of a humpback calf's first year.

Humpback whales are born in January. They weigh nearly 3,000 pounds when they're born. That's heavier than a car! A calf is born tail first. It rolls around like a barrel. But its mother quickly holds it with her flipper. Then she and another whale push the calf to the water's surface. The calf takes its first breath of air.

A calf takes a breath of air with the help of its mother and another whale from its pod.

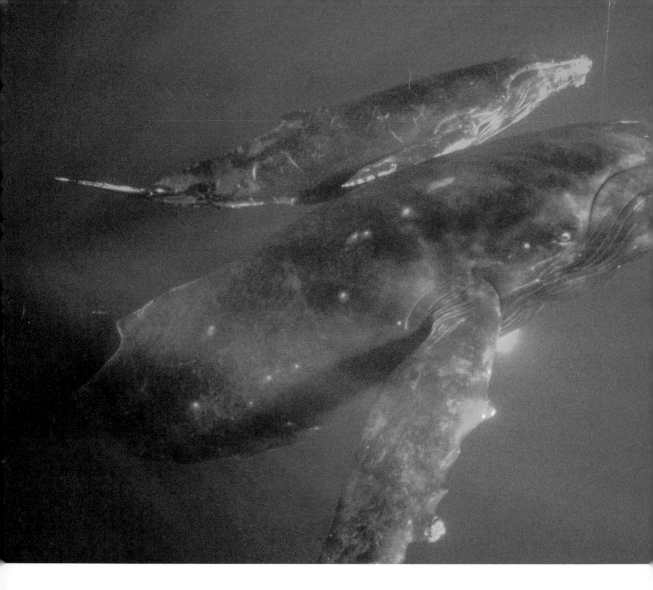

The calf nurses under water, drinking its mother's milk. Baby whales are hungry! Every day, a calf drinks about 130 gallons of milk. In one day, a baby whale drinks more milk than you drink in a year and a half. Every day, a

Humpback whales can grow to be 50 feet long. Their flippers can grow to be 15 feet long!

calf gains about 200 pounds. That's about the same weight as eight bicycles. The mother stays very close to her baby. She touches and strokes it with her flippers. Mother whales keep their calves safe.

A calf must learn to hold its breath and dive. It also practices breaching. When a whale breaches, it leaps out of the water, then comes down with a huge splash. Nobody

A humpback whale breaches.

knows why whales breach. Tiny creatures often attach themselves to whales. Maybe whales breach to knock these creatures off their skin. Or maybe breaching is just fun!

Creatures called barnacles are attached to this gray whale. Inset: a close-up look at barnacles and other creatures on a gray whale.

As the months go by, the adult whales get thin. There's no food for them in warm waters. Since they don't need their blubber to keep warm, their bodies have been using it for food. When humpback calves are a few months old, they're strong enough to swim long

The breath from these humpbacks' blowholes can easily be seen in the warm air of their southern home.

Humpback whales swim at a speed of 2-5 miles per hour.

distances. It's time for the pod to leave the warm waters. They migrate north, where food is easy to find. Day and night, the pod swims slowly through the water. The calves nurse, but the adults hardly ever stop to eat. The trip takes many months.

When the whales reach their northern feeding grounds, they're very hungry. So they eat and eat and EAT! Adult humpbacks can hold up to a ton of food in their stomachs. They may eat as much as 3,000 pounds of plankton every day.

These humpback whales (above and opposite) *are eating.*

The days get shorter and the weather gets colder. Soon it will be time for the humpbacks to migrate to warm waters. Cows will give birth to their calves. New humpback calves will take their first breath, practice diving, and learn to breach. The cycle of life continues.

Only the tails of these humpbacks can be seen as they dive into the water looking for food.

Chapter 5

A humpback whale has died on a beach. Does anyone know why some whales swim onto land?

Whales in Trouble

 Sometimes whales swim onto a beach and get stuck on the sand. This is called stranding. Sometimes a lot of whales strand themselves at the same time. Scientists don't know why this happens. People have a hard time saving stranded whales.

For many years, whales were hunted and killed. In 1985, countries from all over the world decided that hunting whales would be against the law. Even so, Japan, Norway, Iceland, and Russia still kill whales. Some species of whales were hunted so much that they are nearly extinct. That means so many whales have died that not enough calves are

This ship is used for hunting whales.

The right whale was a whale that was hunted almost to extinction.

being born to keep the species alive. The blue whale is almost extinct. There were once more than 200,000 mighty blue whales in the Antarctic alone. Now there are fewer than 9,000 in the whole world. Pollution hurts whales too. If people don't stop killing whales and polluting the oceans, whales may not be able to live anymore.

Chapter 6

Scientists study a humpback whale. Why do you think whales are hard to study?

A Future for Whales

 Whales are hard to study. Big whales can't be kept in zoos or parks. And they're hard to watch under water. But scientists are learning about whales anyway. One discovery is that the fluke, or tail, of each whale has its own special pattern. The pattern is just like a fingerprint. Scientists can tell which whale is which by looking at their flukes. By comparing photographs of whale flukes, scientists are learning how whales travel and live. There's so much to learn about whales. The more scientists discover, the more we know how amazing whales really are.

The flukes on these two humpback whales have different patterns.

The next time you think about the ocean, think about the mighty whales swimming, diving, and breaching. Deep in the ocean are

A pacific white-sided dolphin leaps through the air.

Killer whales swim together in a pod.

whale families who talk, sing, and help each
other and their neighbors. They breathe air
and take care of their young. They are not
much different from you and your family.

On Sharing a Book

As you know, adults greatly influence a child's attitude toward reading. When a child sees you read, or when you share a book with a child, you're sending a message that reading is important. Show your child that reading a book together is important to you. Find a comfortable, quiet place. Turn off the television and limit other distractions like telephone calls.

Be prepared to start slowly. Take turns reading parts of this book. Stop and talk about what you're reading. Talk about the photographs. You may find that much of the shared time is spent discussing just a few pages. This discussion time is valuable for both of you, so don't move through the book too quickly. If your child begins to lose interest, stop reading. Continue sharing the book at another time. When you do pick up the book again, be sure to revisit the parts you have already read. Most importantly, enjoy the book!

Be a Vocabulary Detective

You will find a word list on page 5. Words selected for this list are important to the understanding of the topic of this book. Encourage your child to be a word detective and search for the words as you read the book together. Talk about what the words mean and how they are used in the sentence. Do any of these words have more than one meaning? You will find these words defined in a glossary on page 47.

What about Questions?

Use questions to make sure your child understands the information in this book. Here are some suggestions:

What did this paragraph tell us? What does this picture show? What do you think we'll learn about next? How are whales different from fish? How do whales breathe? What do whales eat? How is a whale family like your family and how is it different? How does echolocation work? What do you think it's like living in the ocean? What is your favorite part of the book? Why?

If your child has questions, don't hesitate to respond with questions of your own like: What do *you* think? Why? What is it that you don't know? If your child can't remember certain facts, turn to the index.

Introducing the Index

The index is an important learning tool. It helps readers get information quickly without searching throughout the whole book. Turn to the index on page 48. Choose an entry such as *blowholes,* and ask your child to use the index to find out how many blowholes a whale has. Repeat this exercise with as many entries as you like. Ask your child to point out the differences between an index and a glossary. (The glossary tells readers what words mean, while the index helps readers find information quickly.)

Where in the World?

Many plants and animals found in the Early Bird Nature Books series live in parts of the world other than the United States. Encourage your child to find the places mentioned in this book on a world map or globe. Take time to talk about climate, terrain, and how your family might live in such places.

All the World in Metric

Although our monetary system is in metric units (based on multiples of 10), the United States is one of the few countries in the world that does not use the metric system of measurement. Here are some conversion activities you and your child can do using a calculator:

WHEN YOU KNOW:	MULTIPLY BY:	TO FIND:
miles	1.609	kilometers
feet	0.3048	meters
inches	2.54	centimeters
gallons	3.787	liters
tons	0.907	metric tons
pounds	0.454	kilograms

Family Activities

Make up a story about a whale. Be sure to include information you've learned in this book. Illustrate your story.

Visit a marine park or zoo to see whales. Are they toothed whales or baleen whales? Can you see their blowholes open and close? How long do they stay under water?

Glossary

baleen (bah-LEEN)—long, furry plates in a whale's mouth that traps food

blowholes—the nostrils on top of whales' heads

blubber—fat

breaching—leaping out of the water

echolocation (eh-koh-loh-KAY-shen)—the use of echoes to find objects

ectotherm (EK-toh-therm)—a cold-blooded animal

endotherm (EN-doh-therm)—a warm-blooded animal

fluke—a whale's tail

migrate—to travel when the seasons change between feeding places and nesting areas

plankton—tiny animals and plants floating in the ocean

pods—whales' family groups

Index

Pages listed in **bold** type refer to photographs.